TUBA ▼ BOOK 1

ESSENTIAL ELEMENTS

A COMPREHENSIVE BAND METHOD

by

Tom C. Rhodes • Donald Bierschenk • Tim Lautzenheiser • John Higgins

Dear Band Student,

Welcome to Essential Elements For Band! We are pleased that you have chosen to play the tuba. With practice and dedication, you'll enjoy a lifetime of music performance.

Best wishes for your musical success!

Linda Petersen, *Editor*

History

OF THE TUBA

Ancient Roman instruments used during military and ceremonial occasions were called "tubas." Actually, these bronze or brass instruments were ancestors to the trumpet.

For centuries, several attempts were made to invent a bass instrument for the brass family. These instruments included the serpent and the ophicleide. The modern tuba, featuring 3-5 valves, was developed in the 1820s. Tuba bells either point straight up or curve forward (a recording bass). In 1898, John Philip Sousa developed the sousaphone for marching bands.

The tuba family includes the BB♭ Tuba (the most common), EE♭ and E♭ Tubas, F and C Tubas. Tubas are the important bass foundation instruments of the concert band. They play bass lines, blend with other instruments and play solos.

Wagner, Mahler, R. Strauss, Vaughan Williams and Hindemith are composers who have included tubas in their writing. Some famous tuba performers are William J. Bell, Harvey Phillips and Roger Bobo.

ISBN 0-7935-1264-6

Copyright © 1991 by HAL LEONARD PUBLISHING CORPORATION
International Copyright Secured   All Rights Reserved

7777 W. BLUEMOUND RD. P.O. BOX 13819 MILWAUKEE, WI 53213

THE BASICS

Posture
Sit on the edge of your chair, and always keep your:
- Spine straight and tall
- Shoulders back and relaxed
- Feet flat on the floor

Breathing & Air Stream
Breathing is a natural thing we all do constantly. To discover the correct air stream to play your instrument:
- Place the palm of your hand near your mouth.
- Inhale deeply through the corners of your mouth, keeping your shoulders steady. Your waist should expand like a balloon.
- Slowly whisper "tah" as you gradually exhale air into your palm.

The air you feel is the air stream. It produces sound through the instrument. Your tongue is like a faucet or valve in that it releases the air stream.

Producing The Essential Tone
"Buzzing" through the mouthpiece produces your tone. The buzz is a fast vibration in the center of your lips. Embouchure (*ahm'-bah-shure*) is your mouth's position on the mouthpiece of the instrument. A good embouchure takes time and effort, so carefully follow these steps for success:

BUZZING
- Moisten your lips.
- Bring your lips together as if saying the letter "m."
- Relax your jaw to separate your upper and lower teeth.
- Form a slightly puckered smile to firm the corners of your mouth.
- Direct a full air stream through the center of your lips, creating a buzz.
- Buzz frequently without your mouthpiece.

MOUTHPIECE PLACEMENT
- Form your "buzzing" embouchure.
- Center the mouthpiece on your lips. Your teacher may suggest a slightly different mouthpiece placement.
- Take a full breath through the corners of your mouth.
- Start your buzz with the syllable "tah." Buzz through the center of your lips keeping a steady, even buzz.
- Your lips provide a cushion for the mouthpiece.

Mouthpiece Work-Outs
Like a physical work out, mouthpiece work-outs may make you dizzy and tired at first. Keep practicing, and you'll see daily improvement.

Hold the mouthpiece on the stem with your thumb and first finger. Carefully form your embouchure and take a deep breath. Begin a steady, even buzz with the syllable "tah." Your mouthpiece work-out looks like this:

For higher tones, make the opening in the center of your lips more firm. For lower tones, slightly relax the opening.

Getting It Together

Step 1 - If you are playing a TUBA, rest it across your lap with the mouthpiece receiver toward you. If you are playing a SOUSAPHONE, place the open circular section over your left shoulder. Rest your right arm comfortably on the tubing.

Step 2 - Carefully twist the mouthpiece to the right into the mouthpiece receiver.

Step 3 - Place your right thumb in the thumb ring. Rest your fingertips on top of the valves, keeping your wrist straight. Your fingers should curve naturally.

Step 4 - For TUBAS, place your left hand on the large tubing next to the bell. Lift the instrument up toward you and rest it in your lap.

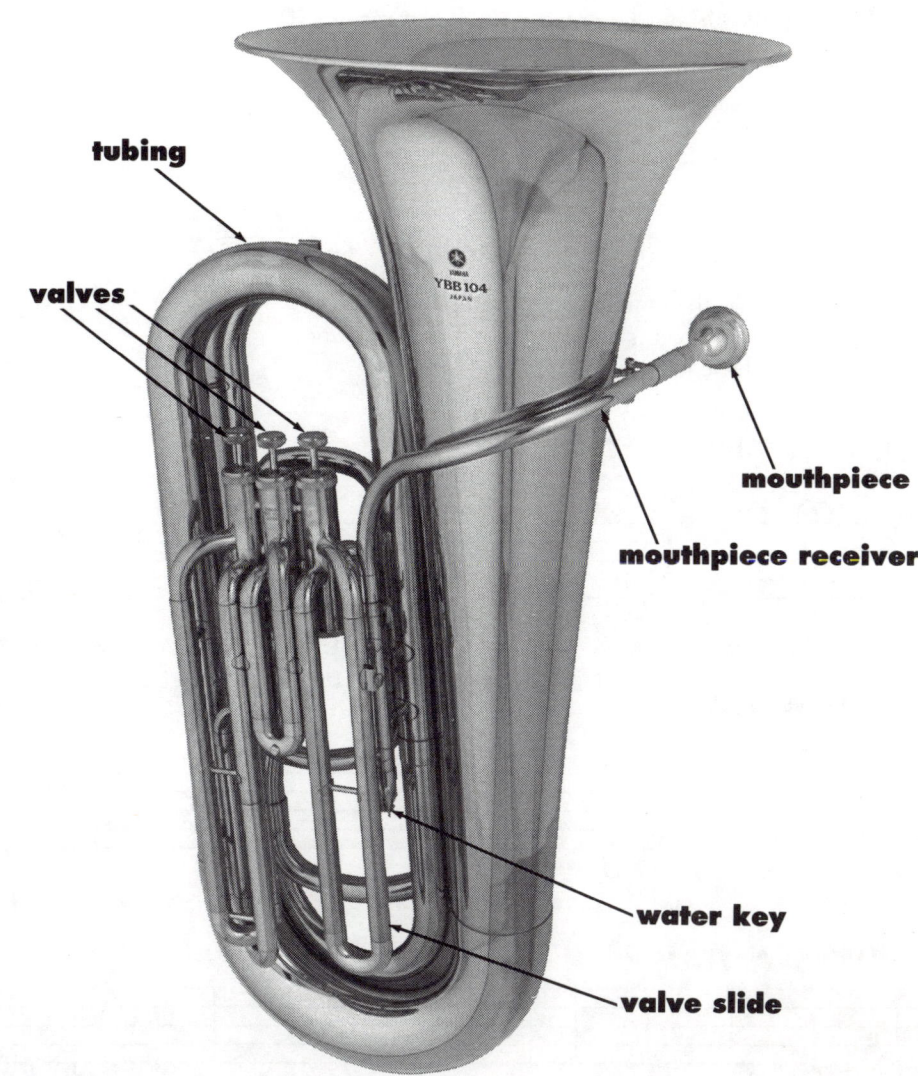

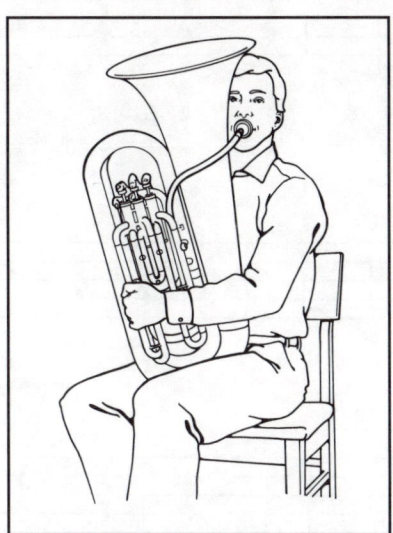

Step 5 - Be sure you can comfortably reach the mouthpiece. Hold the tuba as shown at left:

Let's Play!

This special exercise is just for tuba players. Place your fingers on the valves as shown: ○○○
Begin your steady, even buzz and whisper "tah" to play **F**.
Try this exercise several times.

Beat • The *Pulse* of Music

One beat = tap foot **down** on the number and **up** on the "&." Count and tap when playing or resting.

Count 1 & 2 & 3 & 4 &
Tap   ↓ ↑ ↓ ↑ ↓ ↑ ↓ ↑

Fermata 🠲 Hold the note longer, or until your director tells you to release it.

Staff, Bar Lines & Measures

Bar lines divide the music staff into **measures**. The measures on this page have four beats each.

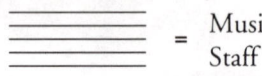

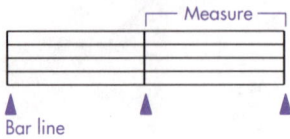

Notes & Rests

Notes tell us how high or low to play *and* how long to play. Notes are placed on a line or space of the music staff.

Rests tell us to count silent beats.

1. COUNT AND PLAY

2. A NEW NOTE

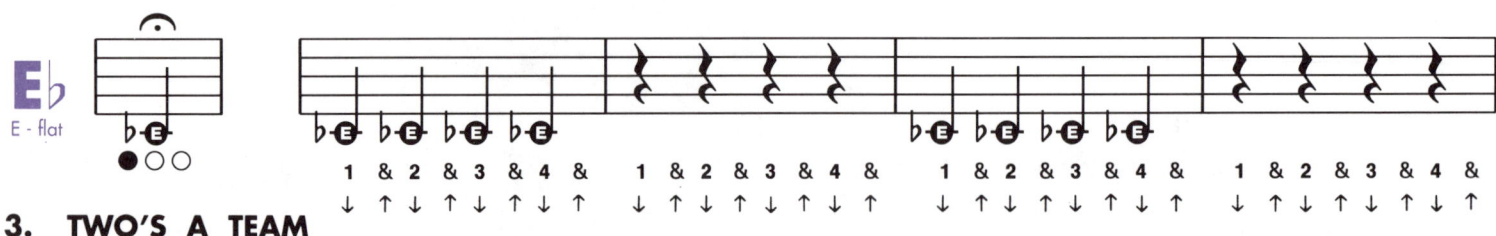

3. TWO'S A TEAM

4. THE NEXT NOTE

5. DOWN AND UP

6. ROLLING ALONG

Go to next line. ▼

Bass Clef

indicates a new line of music and a set of note names.

Time Signature (Meter) 𝄞 4/4

tells us how many beats are in each measure *and* what kind of note gets one beat.

4 – 4 beats per measure
4 – ♩ or 𝄽 gets one beat

Note Names

▲ leger line

Each line and space of the staff has a **note name** that tells us what pitch to play.

Sharp ♯ raises the note and remains in effect for the entire measure. **Flat** ♭ lowers the note and remains in effect for the entire measure. Notes not altered by sharps or flats are called **natural** notes.

NOTE FINGERING REVIEW

F   E♭ (E - flat)   G

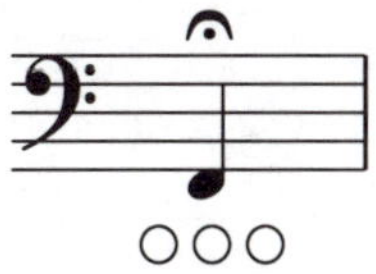

○○○   ♭●○○   ●●○

Double Bar

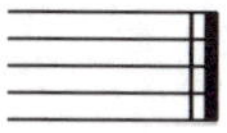

indicates the end of a piece of music.

7. LET'S READ MUSIC!

▼ Play all E's as E - flats.   Double bar ▼

Count 1 & 2 & 3 & 4 &   1 & 2 & 3 & 4 &   1 & 2 & 3 & 4 &   1 & 2 & 3 & 4 &
Tap   ↓ ↑ ↓ ↑ ↓ ↑ ↓ ↑   ↓ ↑ ↓ ↑ ↓ ↑ ↓ ↑   ↓ ↑ ↓ ↑ ↓ ↑ ↓ ↑   ↓ ↑ ↓ ↑ ↓ ↑ ↓ ↑

Repeat Sign 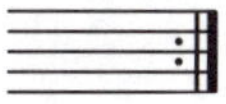   Go back to the beginning and play the line again.

8. COPY CAT

Repeat from beginning ▼

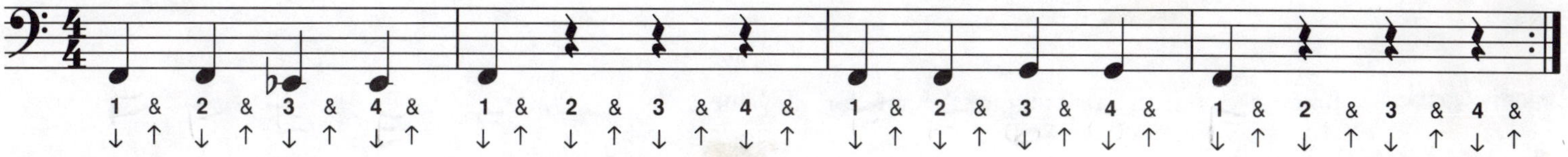

1 & 2 & 3 & 4 &   1 & 2 & 3 & 4 &   1 & 2 & 3 & 4 &   1 & 2 & 3 & 4 &
↓ ↑ ↓ ↑ ↓ ↑ ↓ ↑   ↓ ↑ ↓ ↑ ↓ ↑ ↓ ↑   ↓ ↑ ↓ ↑ ↓ ↑ ↓ ↑   ↓ ↑ ↓ ↑ ↓ ↑ ↓ ↑

9. ROLLING ALONG
Children's Song

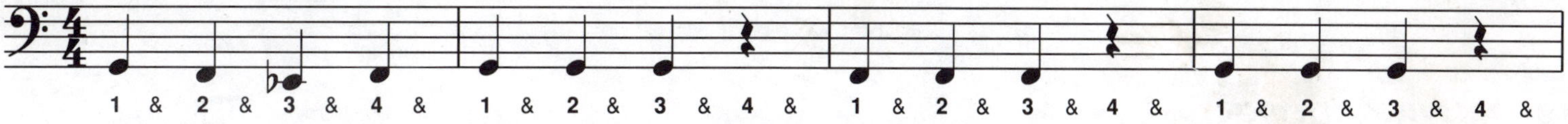

1 & 2 & 3 & 4 &   1 & 2 & 3 & 4 &   1 & 2 & 3 & 4 &   1 & 2 & 3 & 4 &

► Practice this song on your mouthpiece only. Then play it on your instrument.

1 & 2 & 3 & 4 &   1 & 2 & 3 & 4 &   1 & 2 & 3 & 4 &   1 & 2 & 3 & 4 &

10. FIRST FLIGHT

Repeat ▼

1 & 2 & 3 & 4 &   1 & 2 & 3 & 4 &   1 & 2 & 3 & 4 &   1 & 2 & 3 & 4 &

11. ESSENTIAL ELEMENTS QUIZ   Complete the note names before you play.

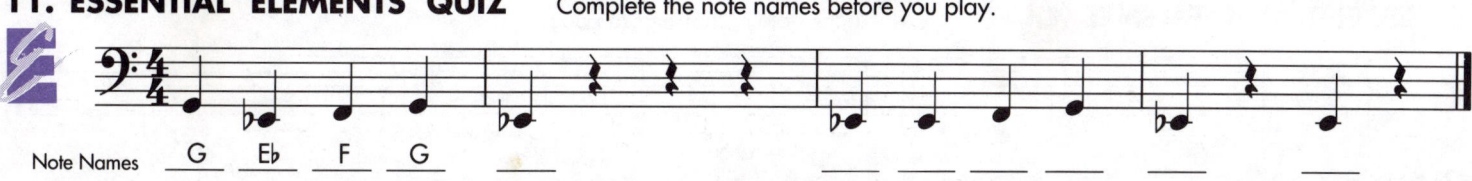

Note Names   G   E♭   F   G   ___   ___   ___   ___   ___   ___   ___   ___

Half Note 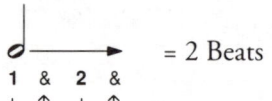 = 2 Beats

Half Rest 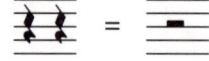 = 2 Silent Beats

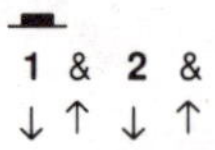

12. RHYTHM RAP Count aloud while clapping and tapping.

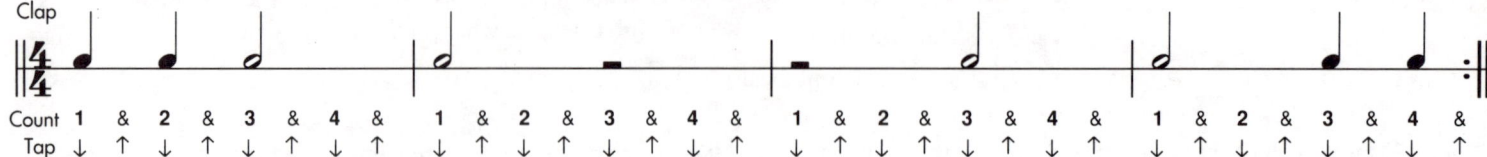

13. THE HALF COUNTS

14. A NEW NOTE

15. MOVING AROUND

16. ANOTHER NEW NOTE

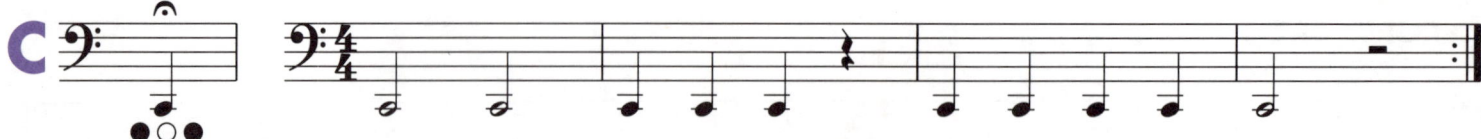

Breath Mark ’ Take a deep breath after you play the note for full value.

17. WALKING

18. MOVING DOWN

19. GO TELL AUNT RHODIE American Folk Song

▶ Practice this song on your mouthpiece only. Then, play it on your instrument.

20. ESSENTIAL ELEMENTS QUIZ Write in the note names before you play.

Note Names

29. EASY STREET

▶ Correct posture improves your sound. Always sit straight and tall.

30. JUMP ROPE

Theory **Harmony** Two or more different notes played or sung at the same time. A duet is a composition for two players. Practice this duet with a friend, and listen to the harmony.

31. LONDON BRIDGE - Duet

English Folk Song

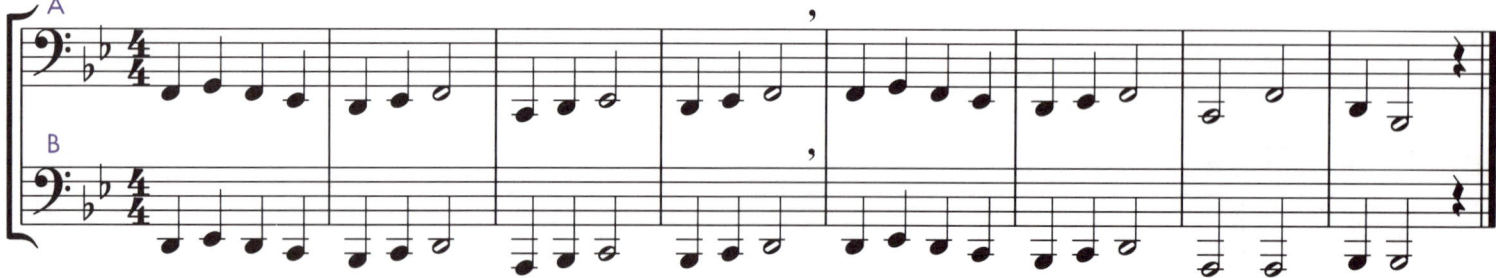

32. POLLY WOLLY DOODLE

Dynamics   *f* (*forte*) Play loudly.   *mf* (*mezzo forte*) Play moderately loud.   *p* (*piano*) Play softly.
Always use full breath support to control your tone at all dynamic levels.

33. CLAP LOUDLY

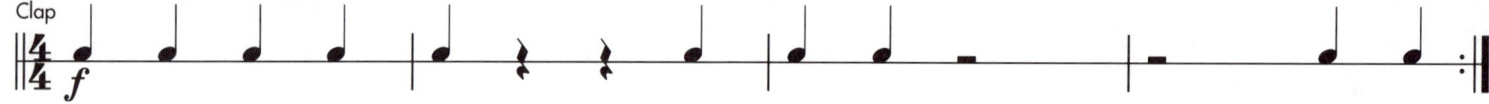

34. CLAP SOFTLY

35. SKIP TO MY LOU

American Folk Song

36. OLD MACDONALD HAD A BAND

▶ Practice this song on your mouthpiece only. Then, play it on your instrument.

37. ESSENTIAL ELEMENTS QUIZ   Write in the note names to complete this sentence.

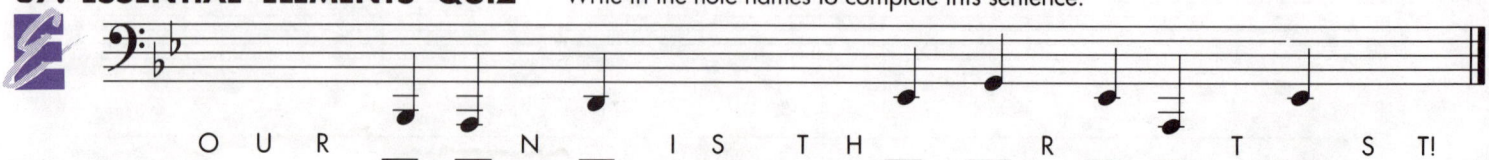

O U R __ __ N I S T H __ __ R __ __ T S T!

Time Signature (Meter)
2 – 2 beats per measure
4 – ♩ or 𝄽 gets one beat

Conducting

Practice conducting this two-beat pattern.

45. RHYTHM RAP

46. OLD JOE CLARK

Count and clap before you play.

American Folk Song

History One of the world's greatest composers, **Ludwig van Beethoven** (1770-1827), became completely deaf in 1802. Although he could not hear his music like we do, he could "hear" it in his mind. The theme of his last Symphony (No. 9) is called "Ode To Joy." It was composed to the text of a poem by German writer Johann von Schiller. "Ode To Joy" was featured in concerts celebrating the reunification of Germany in 1990.

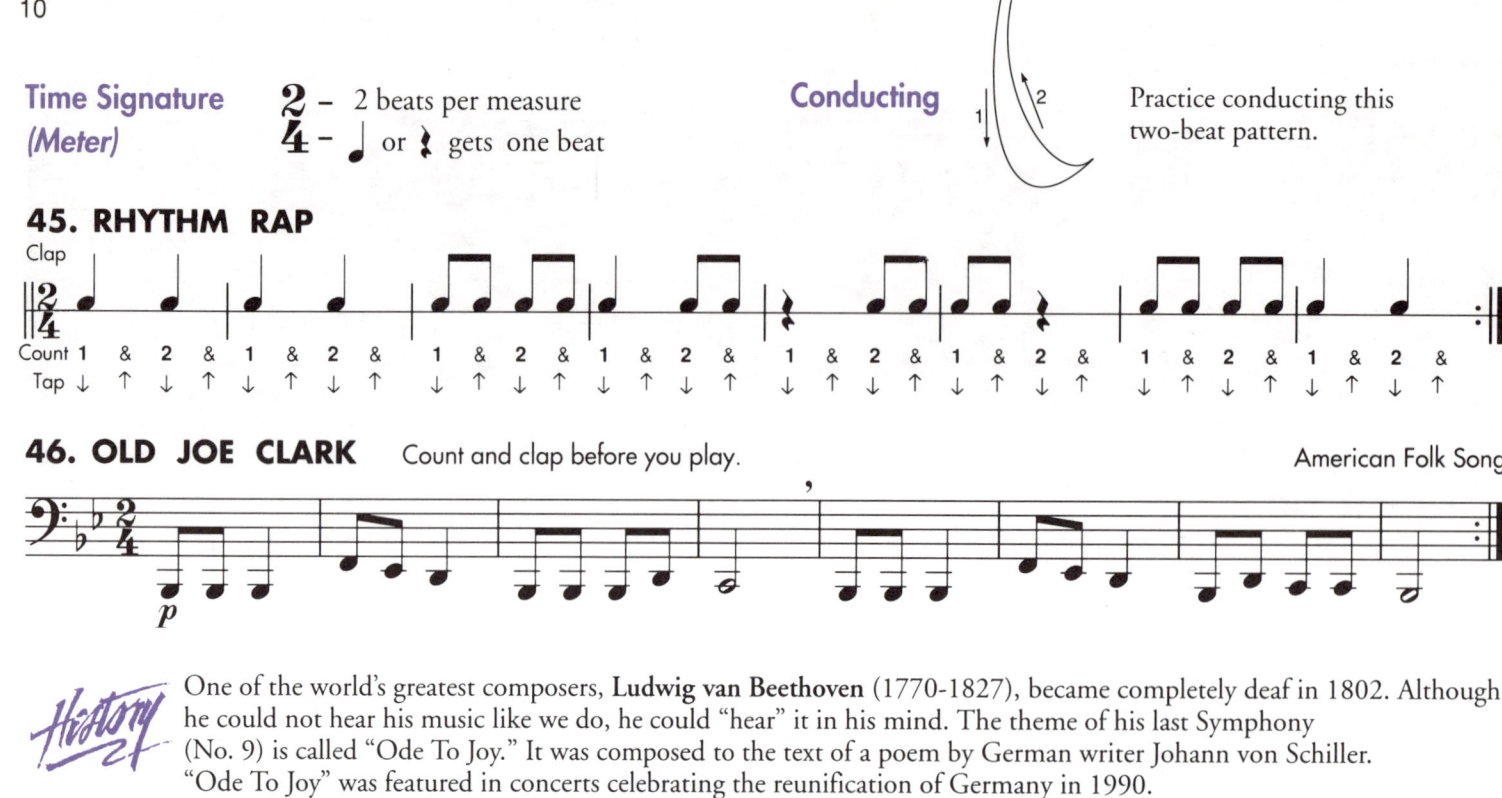

47. ODE TO JOY

Ludwig van Beethoven

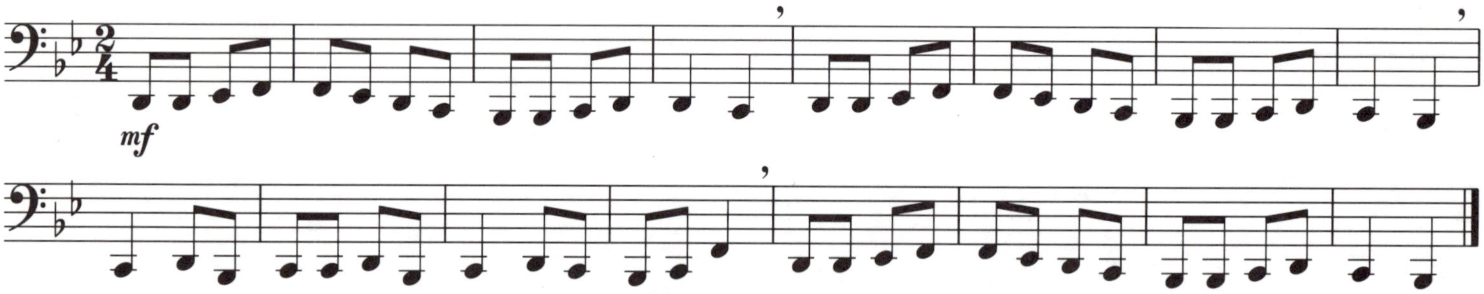

48. HEY, HO! NOBODY'S HOME

Traditional

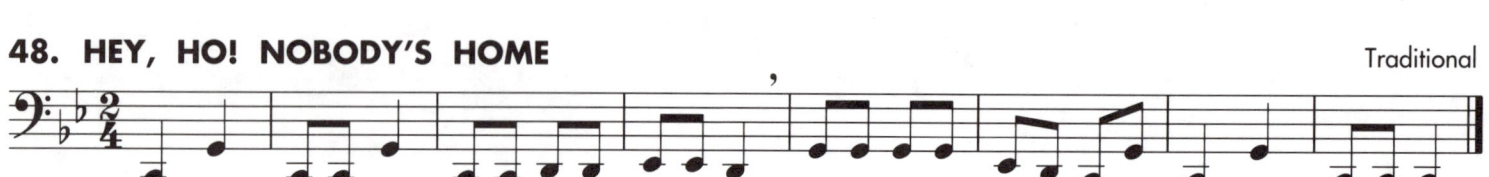

Dynamics
crescendo (*cresc.*) — Gradually increase volume.
decrescendo (*decresc.*) — Gradually decrease volume.

49. CLAP THE DYNAMICS

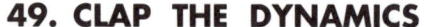

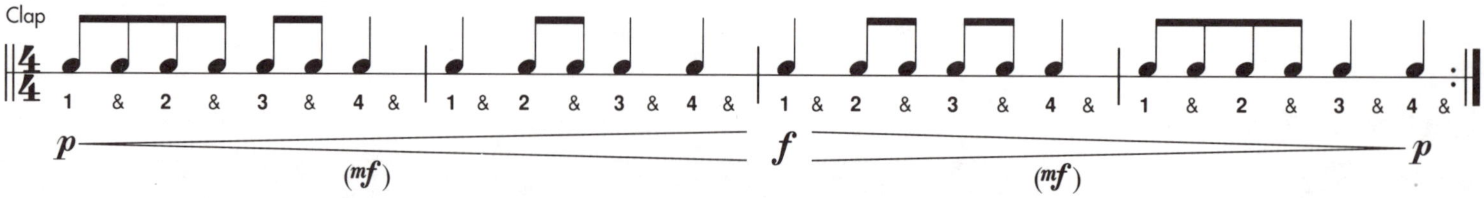

Warm-up Warming up is the proper way to begin a successful performance. After assembling your instrument, carefully set your embouchure. Start your warm-up by playing long tones in the middle register. Then play lower notes, and gradually move into higher notes using easy fingering patterns. Proper breathing and posture are always important.

50. WARM - UP CHORALE #1

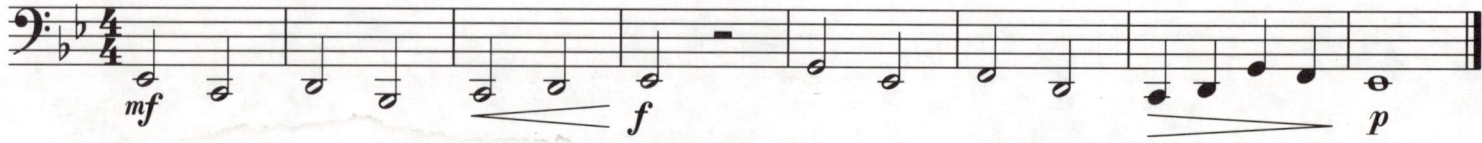

51. MICHAEL ROW YOUR BOAT ASHORE - Duet
American Folk Song

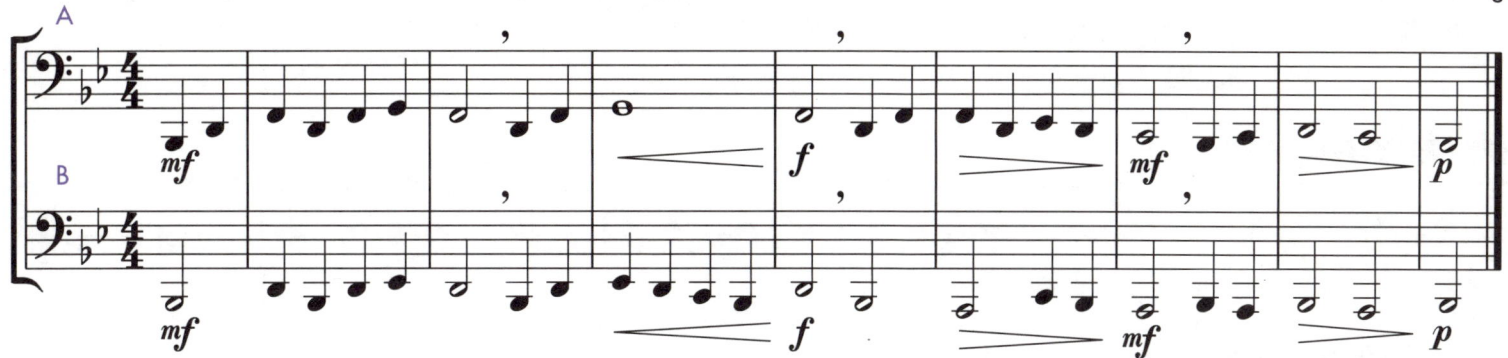

Tie  A curved line that connects notes of the **same** pitch. Play for the combined counts of the tied notes.

52. FIT TO BE TIED

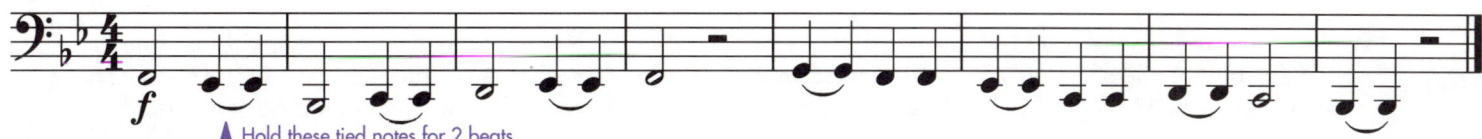

▲ Hold these tied notes for 2 beats.

53. ALOUETTE
French Folk Song

▲ Hold these tied notes for 3 beats.

Dotted Half Note

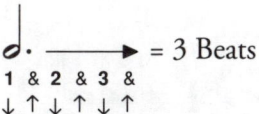 = 3 Beats

 ◄ Dot
A dot adds half the value of the note.

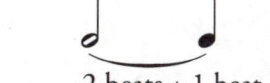
2 beats + 1 beat = 3 beats

54. RETURN TO ALOUETTE'S PLACE
French Folk Song

History American composer **Stephen Collins Foster** (1826-1864) wrote 189 songs, many of which became classic American folk songs. Most of Foster's songs were published shortly before the American Civil War (1860-1865). His works include "Oh, Susanna," "My Old Kentucky Home" and "Camptown Races."

55. CAMPTOWN RACES
Stephen Collins Foster

Tempo The speed of music. Tempo markings are usually written in Italian and are found above the staff.

    Andante — Slow walking tempo   **Moderato** — Moderate tempo   **Allegro** — Fast bright tempo

56. ESSENTIAL ELEMENTS QUIZ
Moderato

Where is beat 4? ▲

12

Time Signature (Meter) — 3/4 — 3 beats per measure — ♩ or 𝄽 gets one beat

Conducting — Practice conducting this three-beat pattern.

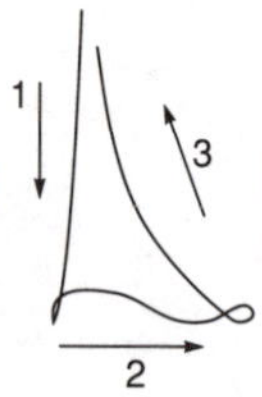

57. RHYTHM RAP

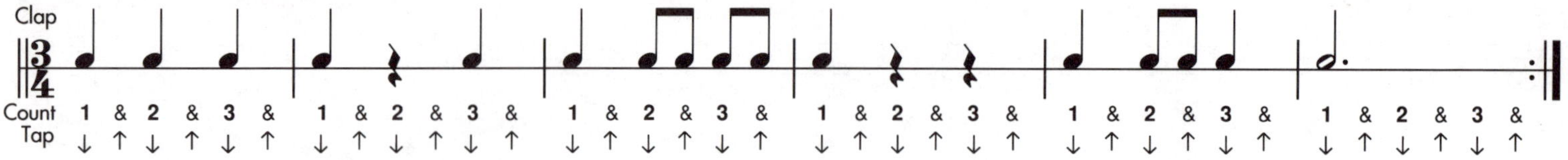

58. A MINI WALTZ — Count and clap before you play.
Moderato

▶ Keep your cheeks in and direct a full air stream through your instrument.

History: Norwegian composer **Edvard Grieg** (1843-1907) wrote *Peer Gynt Suite* in 1875 for a play by Henrik Ibsen. Music used in plays, films, radio and television is called **incidental music**. *Peer Gynt Suite* was written the year before the telephone was invented by Alexander Graham Bell. "Morning" is a melody from the first movement of the *Peer Gynt Suite*.

59. MORNING
Edvard Grieg

Accent ♩ or ♩ Emphasize the note.

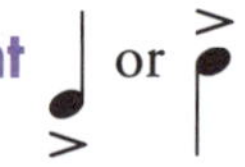

60. ACCENT YOUR TALENT

History: **Latin American music** combines the folk music from South and Central America, the Caribbean Islands, American Indian, African, Spanish and Portuguese cultures. In this diverse music, melodies feature a lively accompaniment by drums, maracas and claves. Latin American music continues to influence jazz, classical and popular styles of music. This melody, also known as *Chiapanecas*, is a popular children's dance and game song in Latin American countries.

61. MEXICAN CLAPPING SONG
Latin American Folk Song

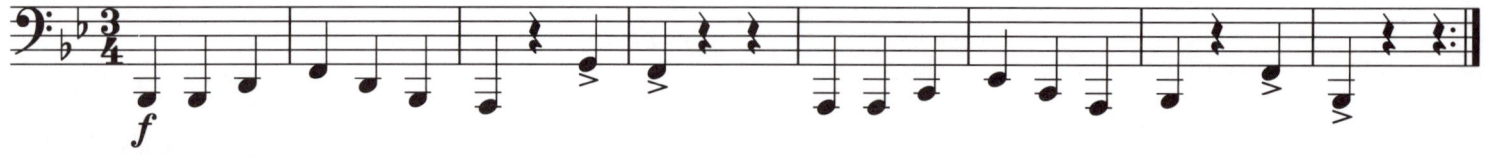

62. RISING MUFFINS

A♭ A - flat

▲ Remember the ♭ applies to all A's in this measure.

63. ESSENTIAL ELEMENTS QUIZ - RUSSIAN DANCE

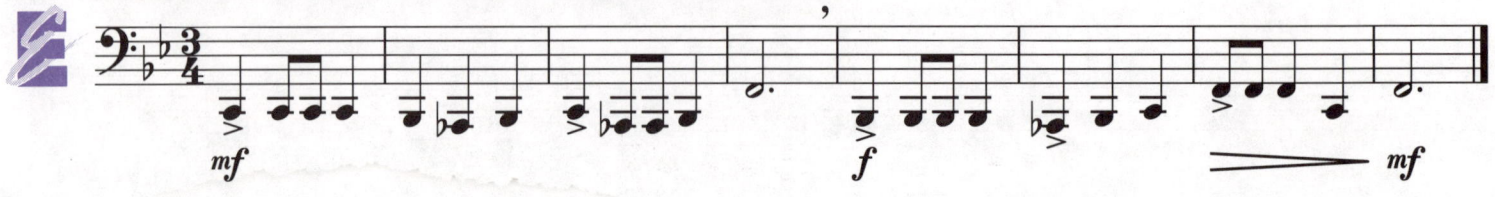

1st and 2nd Endings  Play the 1st ending the 1st time through. Then, repeat the same section of music, skip the 1st ending and play the 2nd ending.

64. CIRCUS WALTZ

65. HATIKVAH
Hebrew Folk Song

History **Japanese folk music** has origins in ancient China. "Sakura, Sakura" was written for the koto, a 13-string instrument that is over 4000 years old. The unique sound of this ancient Japanese song results from the pentatonic, or five-note sequence used in this tonal system.

66. SAKURA, SAKURA - Full Band Arrangement
(Song of the Blooming Cherry Tree)
Japanese Folk Song
Arr. by John Higgins

67. THE BIG AIR STREAM

▲ Play B♭'s, E♭'s, and all A's as A♭'s in this key signature.

68. JOLLY OLD ST. NICK - Duet

69. TECHNIQUE TRAX
Andante

► Keep fingers on top of the valves arched naturally.

Theory — **Theme and Variations** — A musical form where a theme is followed by variations, or different versions, of the theme. A theme is usually a short melody.

70. VARIATIONS ON A FAMILIAR THEME

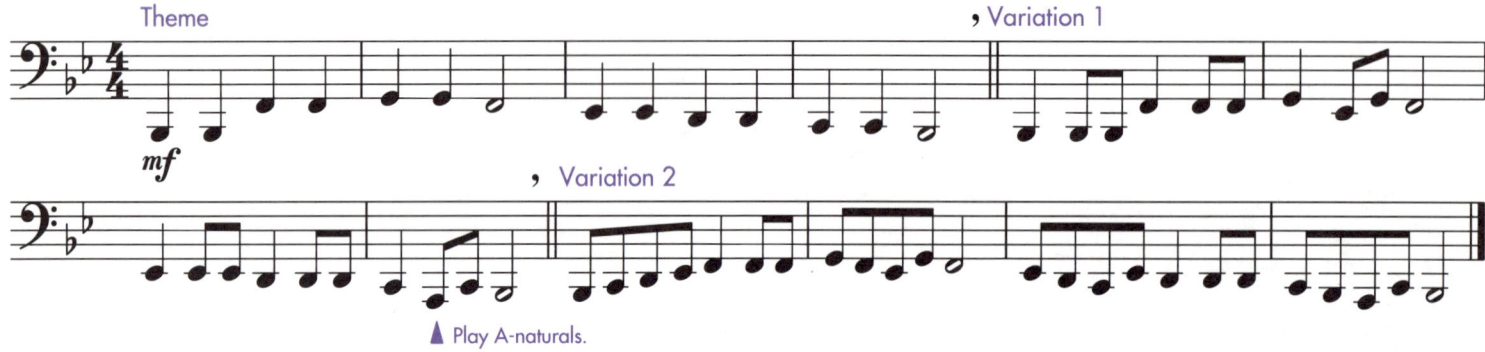

▲ Play A-naturals.

D.C. al Fine — Play until you see the *D.C. al Fine*. Then, go back to the beginning and play until you see *Fine* (fee'-nay). *D.C.* is the Latin abbreviation for *Da Capo*, or return to the beginning. *Fine* is Latin for "the finish."

71. BANANA BOAT SONG
Latin American Folk Song

72. THE LITTLE MUSIC BOX

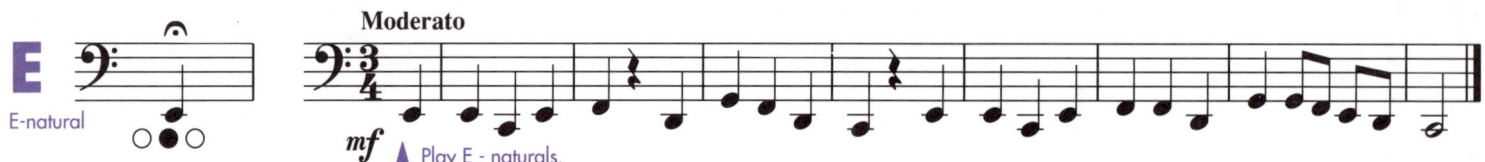

E-natural

▲ Play E - naturals.

History — **Black American spirituals** originated in the 1700's. As one of the largest categories of true American folk music, these melodies were sung and passed on for generations without being written down. Black and white people worked together to publish the first spiritual collection in 1867, four years after The Emancipation Proclamation was signed into law. "What A Morning" is a famous Black American spiritual.

73. ESSENTIAL ELEMENTS QUIZ - WHAT A MORNING
Black American Spiritual

Slur  A curved line that connects notes of **different** pitches. Tongue only the first note of each group of notes connected by a slur.

74. SMOOTH OPERATOR

p ▲ Slur 2 notes. Tongue the first note. Play the next note without tongueing.

75. GLIDING ALONG

mf ▲ Slur 4 notes. Tongue only the first note of notes connected by a slur.

History **Ragtime** is an American music style (1896-1918) that was popular before World War I. It uses early forms of jazz rhythms. Scott Joplin wrote many ragtime piano pieces. The trombones will now learn a *glissando*, a technique used in ragtime and other styles of music.

76. TROMBONE RAG
Allegro

Phrases Musical sentences that are usually 2 or 4 measures long. Try to play phrases in one breath.

77. THE COLD WIND
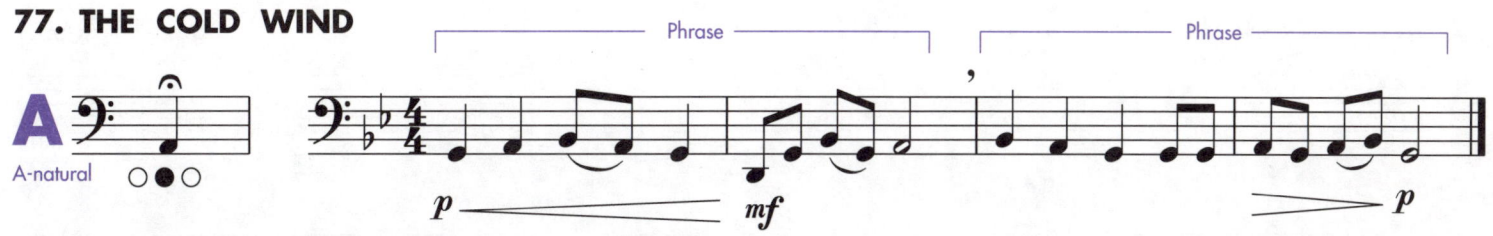

A-natural

Multiple Measures Rest 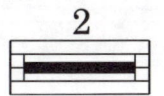 The large number tells you how many measures to count and rest. Count each measure in sequence: **1** 2 3 4 | **2** 2 3 4

78. SATIN LATIN

▲ Play B♭'s, E - naturals, and A - naturals.

History German composer **Johann Sebastian Bach** (1685-1750) wrote hundreds of choral and instrumental works. He was a master teacher, organist and famous improviser. Bach had 21 children, many of whom became famous composers. He wrote this Minuet, or dance in 3/4 time, as a piano teaching piece.

79. ESSENTIAL ELEMENTS QUIZ - MINUET - Duet
Johann Sebastian Bach

80. WARM - UP CHORALE #2 - FINLANDIA
Jean Sibelius

Always check the key signature.

History: Austrian composer **Franz Peter Schubert** (1797-1828) was a great composer of songs, symphonies and piano works. He wrote three military marches for piano duet. "March Militaire" is the introduction and theme from one of these popular marches.

Natural Sign ♮ Cancels a flat ♭ or sharp ♯. A natural sign remains in effect for the entire measure.

81. MARCH MILITAIRE
Franz Schubert

82. MY BONNIE LIES OVER THE OCEAN
Scottish Folk Song

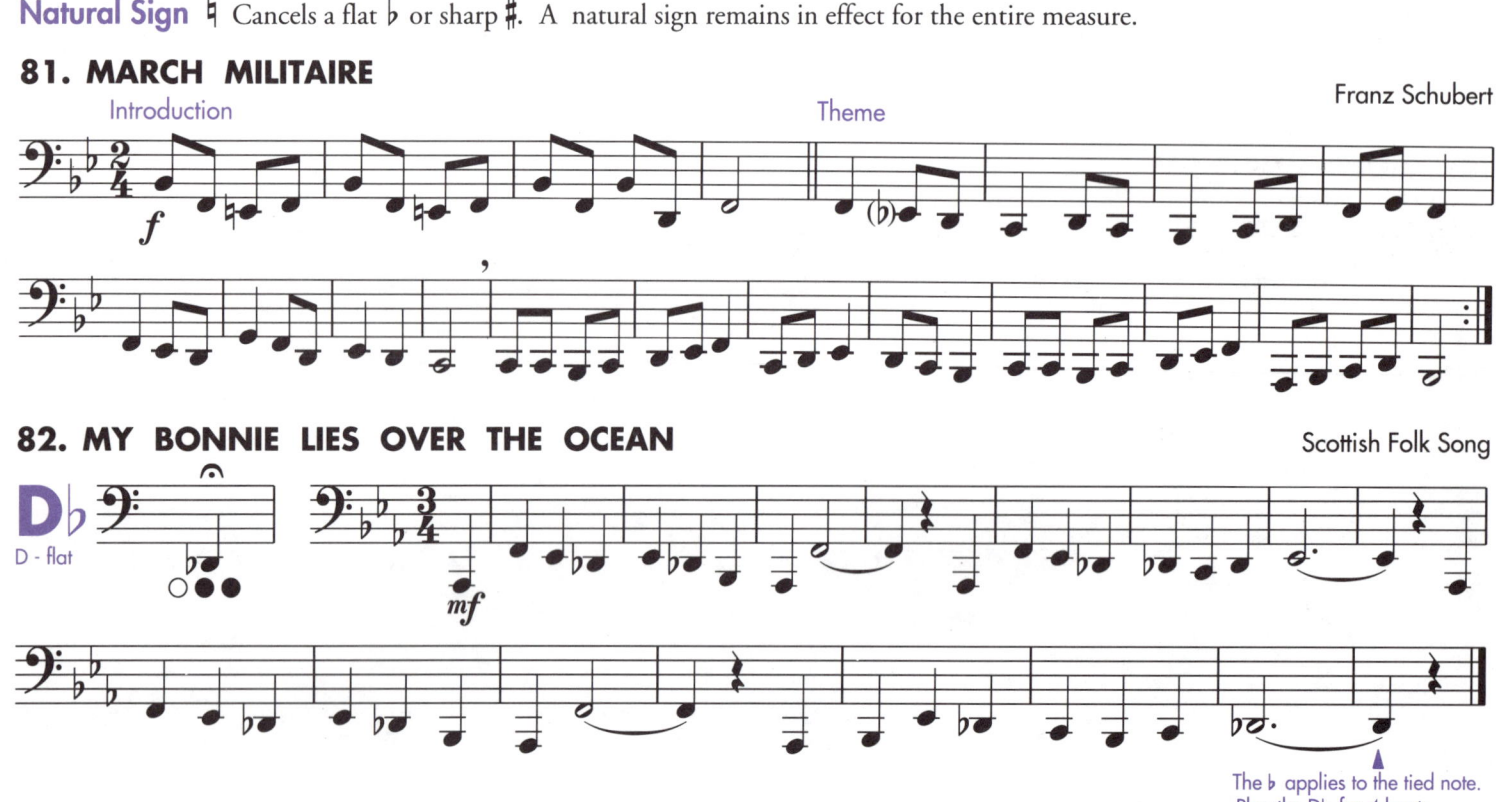

The ♭ applies to the tied note. Play the D♭ for 4 beats.

History: **Blues** is a form of Black American folk music related to jazz. Boogie-woogie is a blues style first recorded by pianist Clarence "Pine Top" Smith in 1928, one year after Charles Lindbergh's solo flight across the Atlantic. Blues music has altered notes and is usually written in 12 bars, like "Bottom Bass Boogie."

83. BOTTOM BASS BOOGIE - Duet

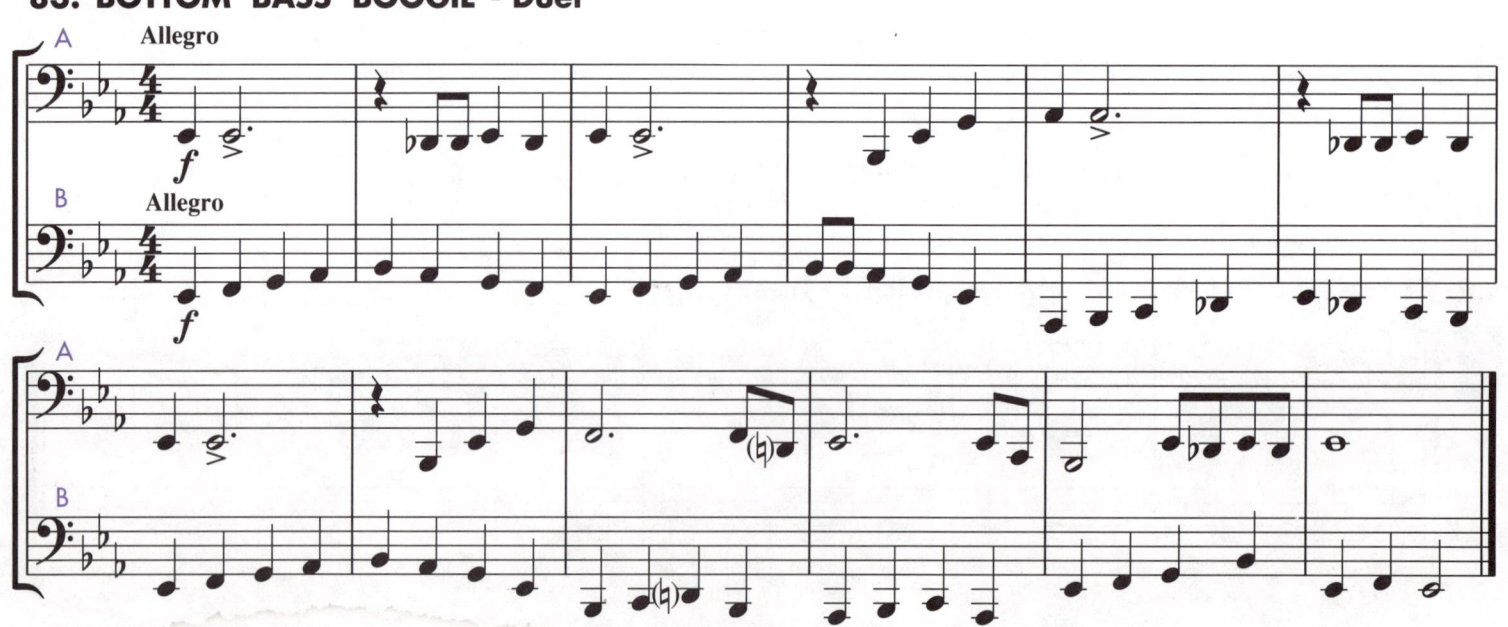

Dotted Quarter Note / Eighth Note

84. RHYTHM RAP

85. THE DOT ALWAYS COUNTS

86. AULD LANG SYNE
Scottish Folk Song

87. SCARBOROUGH FAIR
English Folk Song

88. ALL THROUGH THE NIGHT

History: Bohemian composer **Antonin Dvořák** (1841-1904) wrote his famous **Symphony From The New World** in 1894 while living in New York. Many melodies from this work are based on American folksongs and spirituals. This is the largo (very slow tempo) theme.

89. ESSENTIAL ELEMENTS QUIZ - THEME FROM NEW WORLD SYMPHONY
Antonin Dvořák

Great musicians give encouragement to their fellow performers. Clarinetists will now learn a challenging slur pattern, called "Grenadilla Gorilla Jumps." Many clarinets are made of grenadilla wood. Brass players will learn lip slurs, a new warm-up pattern. The success of your band depends on everyone's help and patience. Let's play our best as these sections advance their musical technique.

Lip Slurs Notes that are slurred without changing valves are called lip slurs. Brass players practice lip slurs to develop a stronger embouchure and increase range. Add this pattern to your daily warm-up:

SPECIAL TUBA EXCERCISE

90. GRENADILLA GORILLA JUMP #1

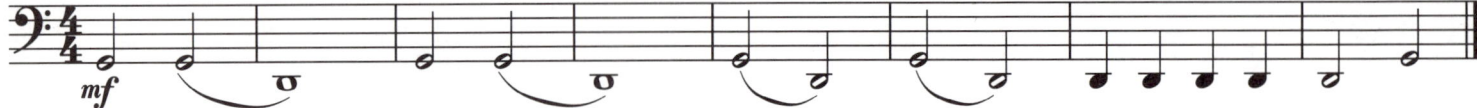

91. JUMPIN' UP AND DOWN

Play A♮'s.

92. GRENADILLA GORILLA JUMP #2

93. JUMPIN' FOR JOY

Theory **Interval** The distance between two notes. Starting with "1" on the lower note, count each line and space between the notes. The number of the higher note is the distance of the interval.

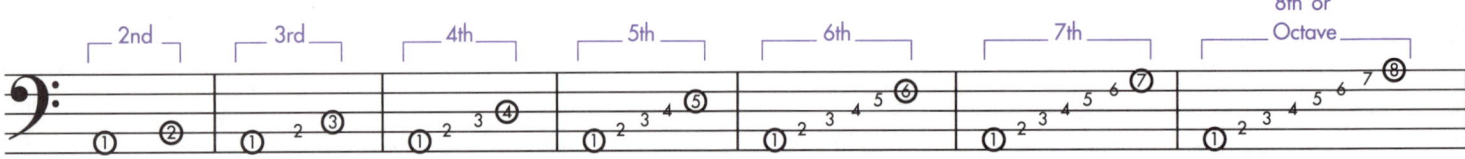

94. GRENADILLA GORILLA JUMP #3

95. JUMPIN' JACKS

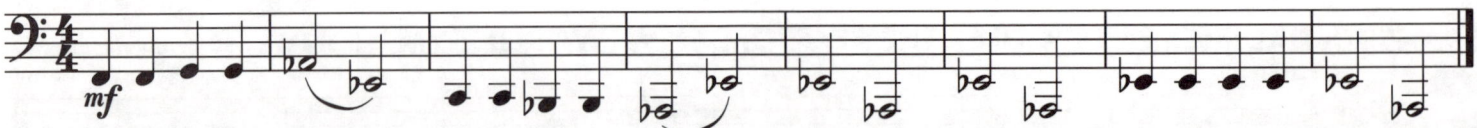

96. ESSENTIAL ELEMENTS QUIZ   Write in the numbers of the intervals. Remember to count **up** from the lowest note.

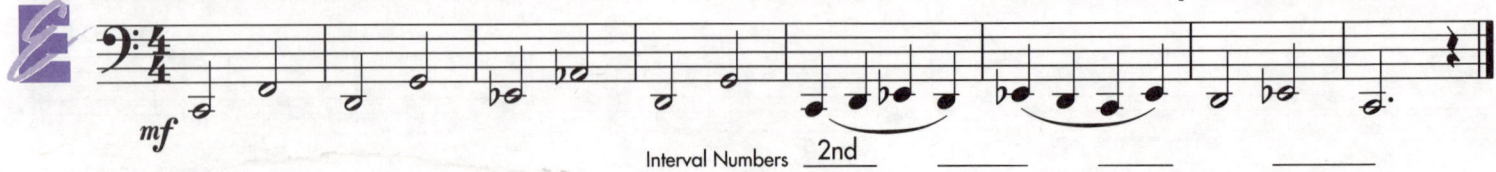

Interval Numbers   2nd

97. GRENADILLA GORILLA JUMP #4

98. THREE IS THE COUNT
Draw in the bar lines before you play.

99. DIXIE
Dan Emmett

▲ Play B♭'s, E♭'s, and A♭'s.

100. GRENADILLA GORILLA JUMP #5
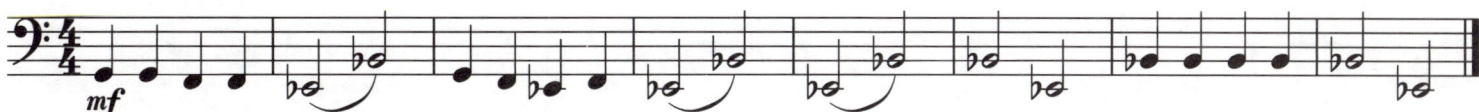

101. TECHNIQUE TRAX

Theory Trio A composition for three players. Practice this trio with two other players and listen for 3-part harmony.

102. KUM BAH YAH - Trio
African Spiritual

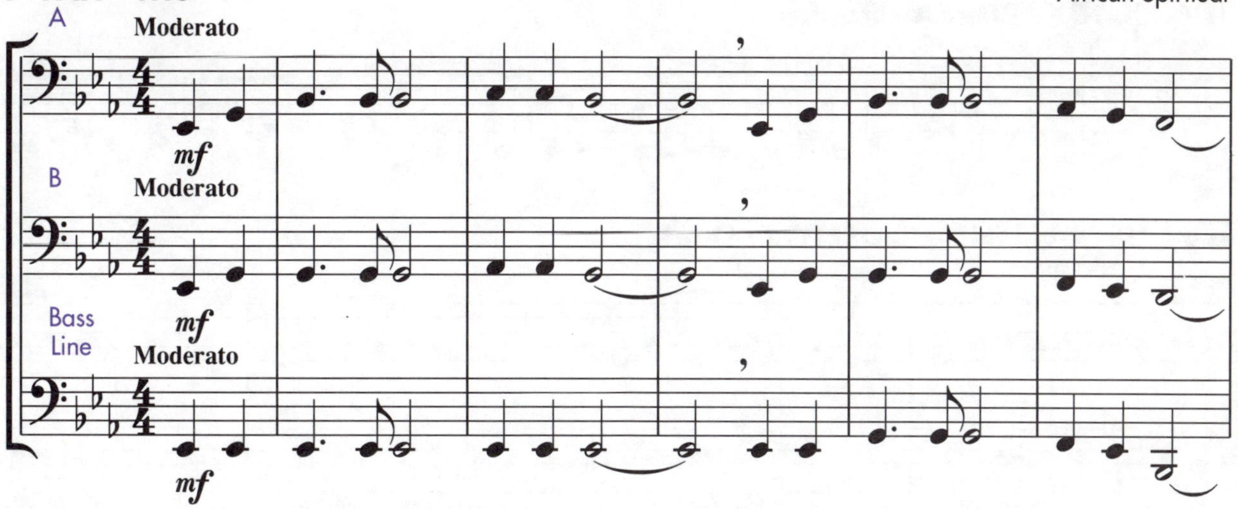

109. EASY JUMPS

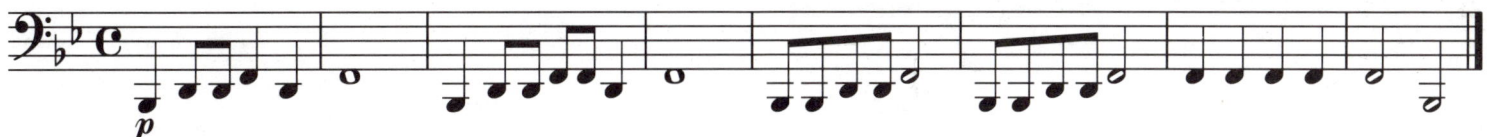

110. TECHNIQUE TRAX

Moderato

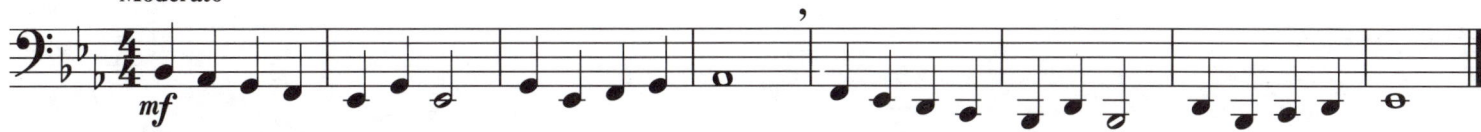

▲ Always check the key signature.

111. GERMAN FOLK SONG

Moderato

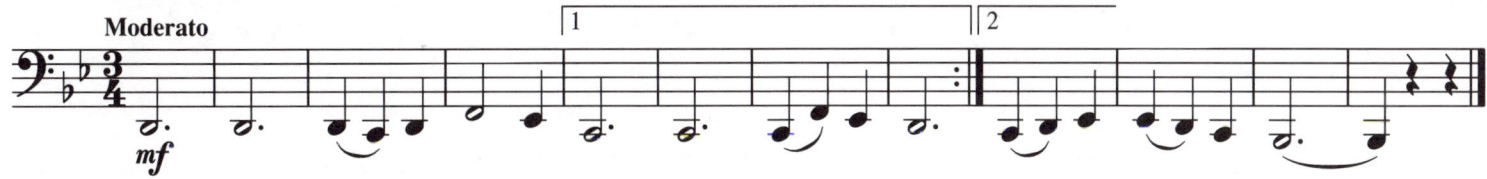

Repeat Sign Repeat the section of music enclosed by the repeat signs

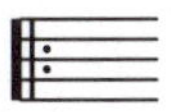

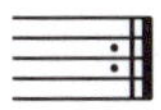

112. WHEN THE SAINTS GO MARCHIN' IN

American Folk Song

Allegro

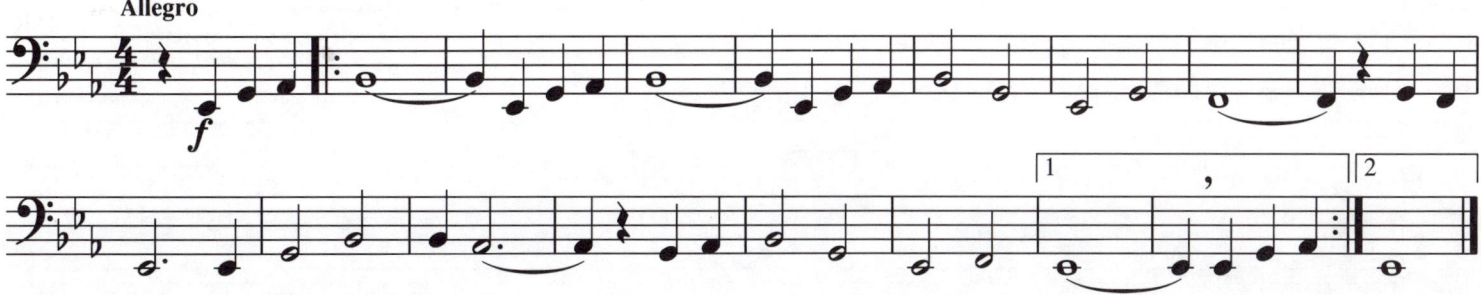

113. LOWLAND GORILLA WALK

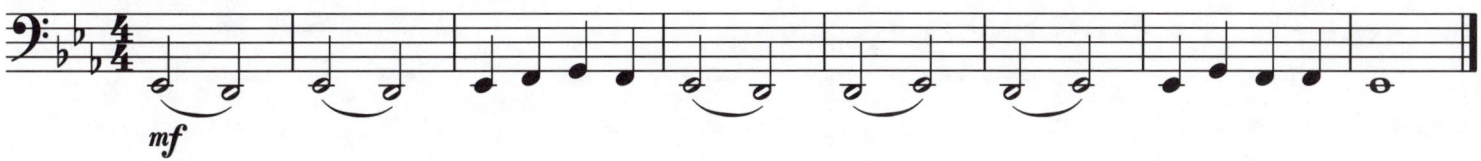

114. SMOOTH SAILING

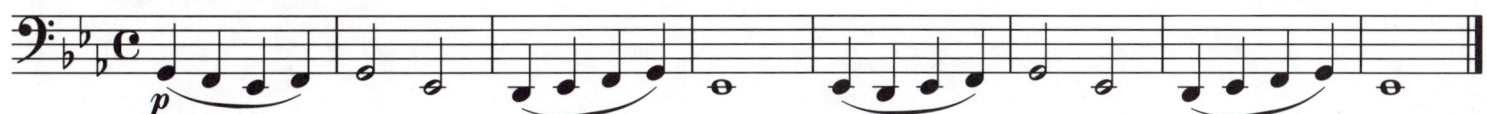

115. MORE EASY JUMPS

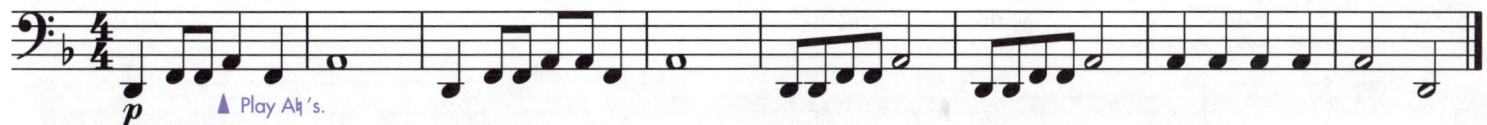

▲ Play A♮'s.

116. CAREFUL CLARINET COVER

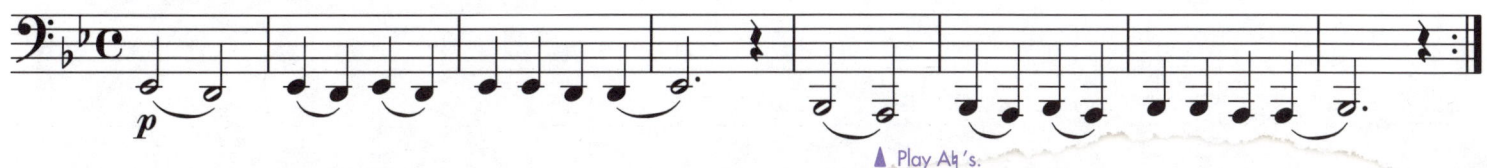

▲ Play A♮'s.

Theory **Scale** A sequence of notes in ascending or descending order. The first and last notes of most scales are the same as the name of the scale. The interval between these two notes is called an **octave**.

121. CONCERT B♭ SCALE   (Your B♭ Scale)   Memorize this exercise.

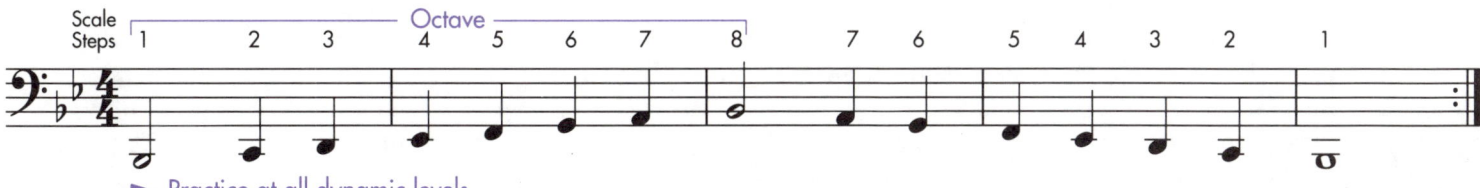

► Practice at all dynamic levels.

Tuning Musicians need to match pitches to play "in tune." We all play the same pitch to check our tuning. A common band tuning note is called **Concert B♭**.

To play Concert B♭ play your written B♭: If you are **above** the pitch (sharp), **pull** the tuning slide **out** slightly.
If you are **below** the pitch (flat), **push** the tuning slide **in** slightly.

Theory **Arpeggio** A sequence of notes from any scale. Your first arpeggio uses the 1st, 3rd, 5th and 8th steps from the Concert B♭ scale.

122. CONCERT B♭ SCALE AND ARPEGGIO   (Your B♭ Scale)   Memorize this exercise.

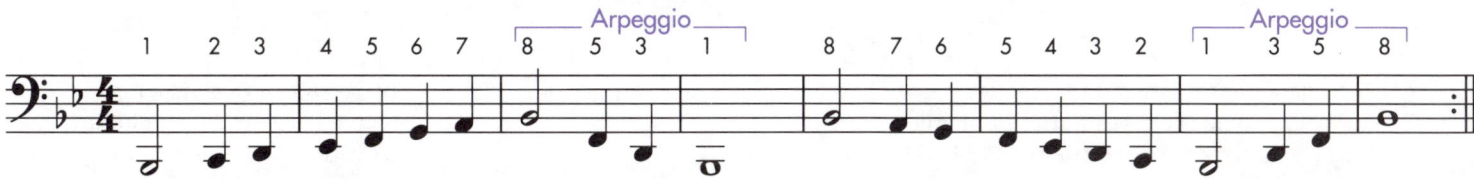

► Practice at all dynamic levels.
► Practice this song on your mouthpiece only. Then, play it on your instrument.

Soli Entire section plays or is featured. In "Carnival Of Venice," listen and name the sections that play the *Soli* at each rehearsal number.

123. CARNIVAL OF VENICE - Full Band Arrangement

Julius Benedict
Arr. by John Higgins

124. A DANCING MELODY

Moderato

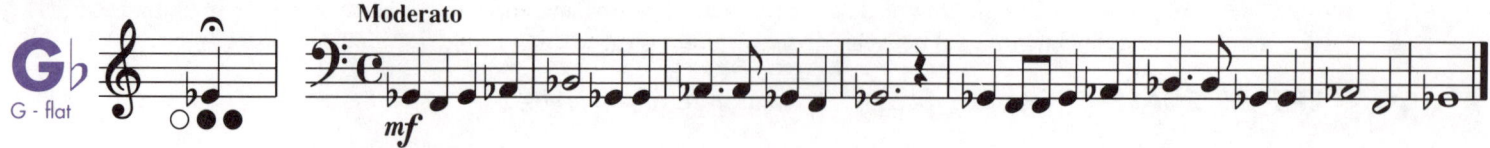

History American composer and conductor **John Philip Sousa** (1854-1932) wrote 136 marches. Known as "The March King," Sousa wrote *The Stars And Stripes Forever, Semper Fidelis, The Washington Post* and many other patriotic pieces. Sousa's band performed all over the country, and his fame helped boost the popularity of bands in America. Here is a melody from his famous *El Capitan* operetta and march.

125. EL CAPITAN

John Philip Sousa

Allegro

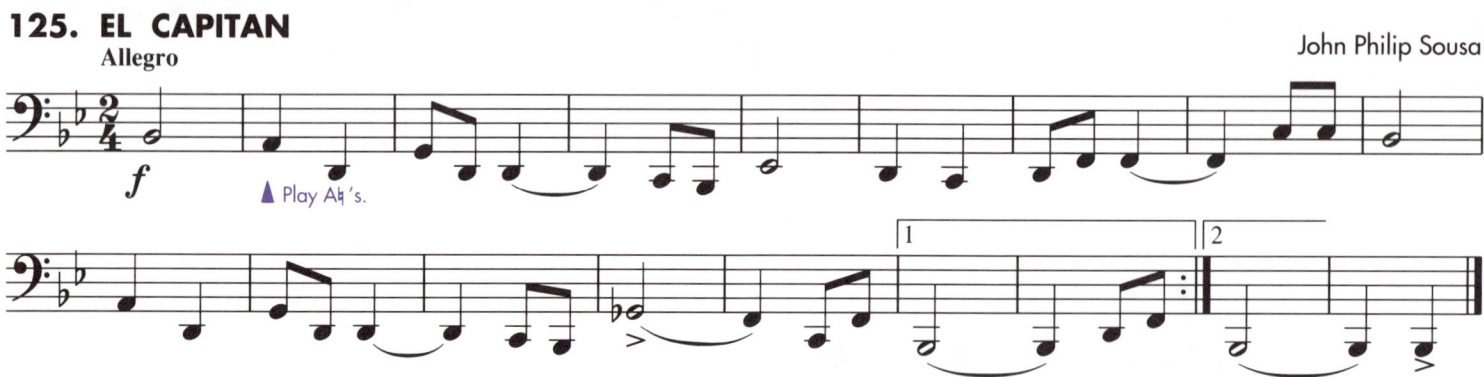

History "O Canada," formerly known as "National Song," was first performed in French Canada during 1880. Robert Stanley Weir translated the English version in 1908. It was officially adopted as the national anthem of Canada in 1980, one hundred years after its premier.

126. O CANADA

Calixa Lavallee,
l'Hon. Judge Routhier
and Justice R.S. Weir

Maestoso (Majestically)

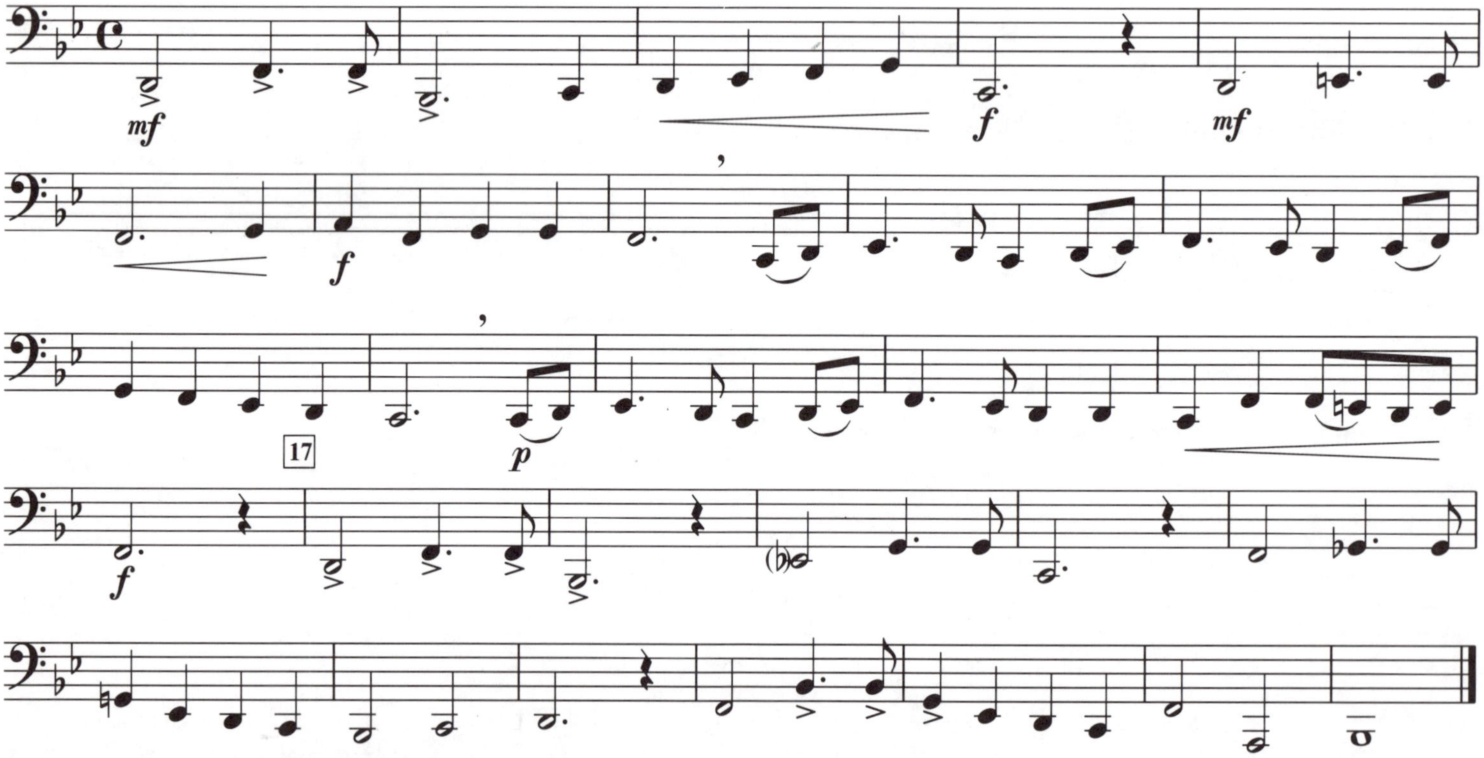

127. ESSENTIAL ELEMENTS QUIZ - METER MANIA #2

Count and clap before playing. Can you conduct this?

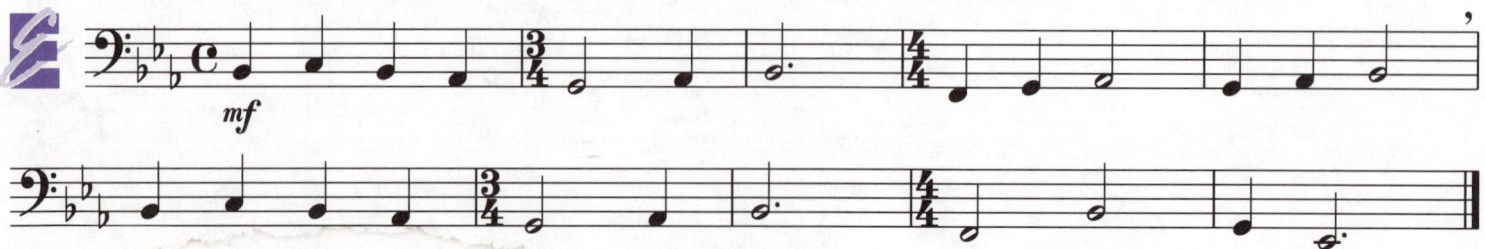

 **Enharmonics** Notes that are written differently but sound the same and are played with the same fingerings. Your fingering chart (pgs. 30-31) shows the enharmonic notes and fingerings for your instrument.

128. SNAKE CHARMER

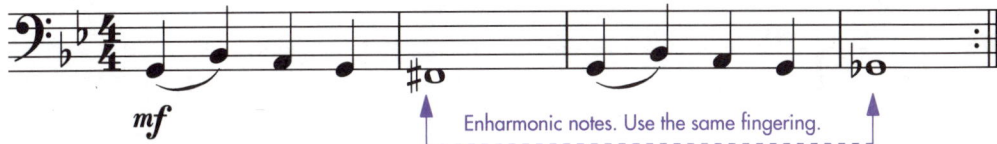

Enharmonic notes. Use the same fingering.

129. CLOSE ENCOUNTERS

Enharmonic notes. Use the same fingering.

130. NOTES IN DISGUISE

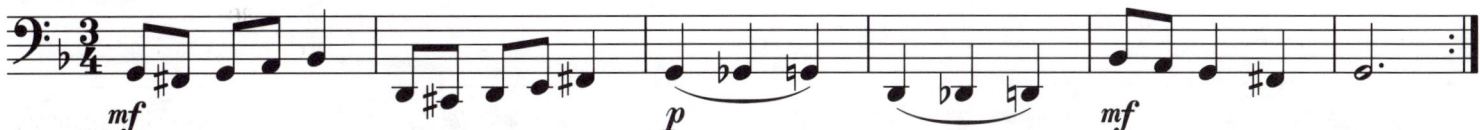

Chromatics Notes that are altered with sharps, flats and naturals. The smallest distance between two notes is called a **half-step**. A scale made up of consecutive half-steps is called a **chromatic scale**.

131. HALF - STEPPIN'

French composer **Camille Saint-Saëns** (1835-1921) wrote many operas, suites, symphonies and chamber works. His famous opera *Samson et Delila* was written in 1877, the same year that Thomas Edison invented the phonograph. "Egyptian Dance" is one of the main opera themes from *Samson et Delila*.

132. EGYPTIAN DANCE

Camille Saint-Saëns

Russian composer **Peter Illyich Tchaikovsky** (1840-1893) wrote 6 symphonies, 3 ballets and hundreds of other works. He was a master at writing popular melodies. His *1812 Overture* and this famous melody from *Capriccio Italien* were both written in 1880, one year after Thomas Edison invented an improved light bulb.

133. CAPRICCIO ITALIEN
Peter I. Tchaikovsky

134. AMERICAN PATROL
F.W. Meacham

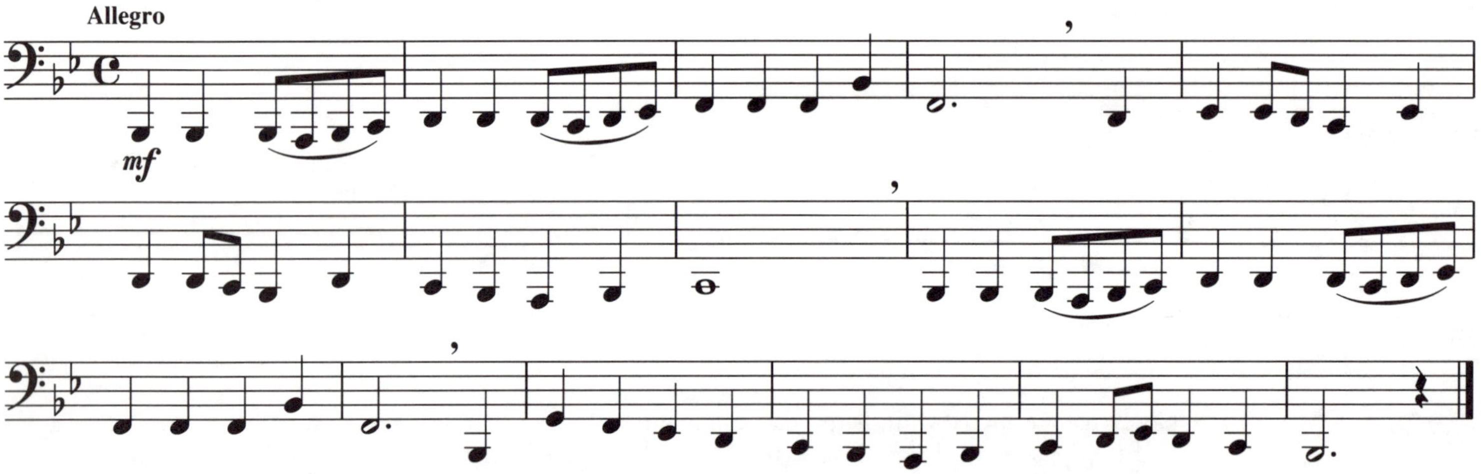

135. WAYFARING STRANGER
Black American Spiritual

136. ESSENTIAL ELEMENTS QUIZ - CONCERT B♭ SCALE COUNTING CONQUEST

Performing for an audience is an exciting part of being involved in music. This solo is based on Johnannes Brahms' **Symphony No. 1 in C Minor, Op. 68**. Brahms was a German composer who lived from 1833-1897. His first symphony was completed in 1876, the same year that Alexander Graham Bell invented the telephone. You and a piano accompanist can perform for the band, your school and at other occasions.

137. THEME FROM SYMPHONY NO. 1 - Solo (E♭ Concert version)

Johannes Brahms
Arr. by John Higgins